I0807992

NFL'S GREATEST PLAYERS

DEFENSIVE PLAYERS

By Kevin Frederickson

Kaleidoscope
Minneapolis, MN

Your Front Row Seat to the Games

This edition first published in 2020 by Kaleidoscope Publishing, Inc.

For information regarding permission, write to
Kaleidoscope Publishing, Inc.
6012 Blue Circle Drive
Minnetonka, MN 55343

Library of Congress Control Number
2019939221

ISBN
978-1-64519-074-5 (library bound)
978-1-64494-171-3 (paperback)
978-1-64519-175-9 (ebook)

Printed in the United States of America.

TABLE OF CONTENTS

CHAPTER 1

A Timely Play

Malcolm Butler stands in the **end zone**. He looks at the Seattle Seahawks offense. He eyes a **wide receiver**. Russell Wilson is Seattle's quarterback. He calls out a play. Butler's New England Patriots are in a tough spot. Seattle needs just one more yard to score.

It is the Super Bowl. New England leads 28–24. Only 27 seconds remain. Seattle could score. Then the Seahawks would probably win.

Wilson gets the ball. He quickly turns his body to his right. He throws the ball. It goes toward Ricardo Lockette.

FUN FACT
The 2014 Seahawks allowed the fewest points in the league.

New England linebacker Rob Ninkovich (50) sacks Seattle quarterback Russell Wilson in Super Bowl XLIX.

Malcom Butler makes the game-winning interception in Super Bowl XLIX.

Butler is right next to Lockette. He doesn't want the receiver to catch the ball. It could mean a touchdown. The ball comes their way. Butler gets in front of Lockette. He grabs the ball. **Interception**!

Butler's teammates start to celebrate. Butler runs forward. He drops to the ground. The Patriots players hug. They throw their hands in the air. They cannot believe what Butler just did. Wilson walks off the field. He looks at the ground. He was sad at how the game ended. The Patriots won 28–24. They were Super Bowl champions!

LEGION OF BOOM

Richard Sherman stands next to a wide receiver. Earl Thomas is behind him. Kam Chancellor stands to his left. Malcolm Smith is closer to the quarterback. These were all Seattle Seahawks defensive players. They were some of the NFL's best. They were known as the Legion of Boom. They helped Seattle make it to multiple Super Bowls in the 2010s.

Football fans love offense. But defense is also important. These players work together to stop the offense. A good defense can change a game. There have been many great defenses in National Football League (NFL) history.

Malcolm Butler (21) celebrates with teammate Julian Edelman after winning the Super Bowl.

Patriots
NFL
Patriots

NFL
Patriots
SUPER BOWL
XLIX

CHAPTER 2

Working Together

The Chicago Bears defense runs onto the field. There are eleven players. They have to work together. Only they can stop the other team's offense.

The 2018 Bears defense was one of the best in the league. It started with the two defensive tackles. They play right next to the ball. Akiem Hicks is on one side. He is a big player. His size makes him tough to block. He runs straight ahead. He has a simple job. He has to stop the player with the ball. He cannot let the player get by.

FUN FACT

The Chicago Bears are known for great linebackers. They have five in the Pro Football Hall of Fame.

Akiem Hicks bears down on Minnesota Vikings quarterback Kirk Cousins in 2018.

Khalil Mack stands to the right of Hicks. He is ready to take off. The ball is **snapped**. Mack **sprints** past the offensive lineman. He sees the quarterback. Slam! Mack throws him to the ground. Players like Mack have to be fast. They can stop the offense quickly.

Roquan Smith stands behind Hicks. He's listening to what the coach says. The coach tells him how the defense should line up. Smith yells out to his teammates. Then the ball is snapped. Smith watches where the ball goes. Smith is a linebacker. These players lead the defense. They call out plays and do many other things.

An outside linebacker, Khalil Mack often plays on the line to rush the passer.

WHERE DEFENSIVE PLAYERS LINE UP

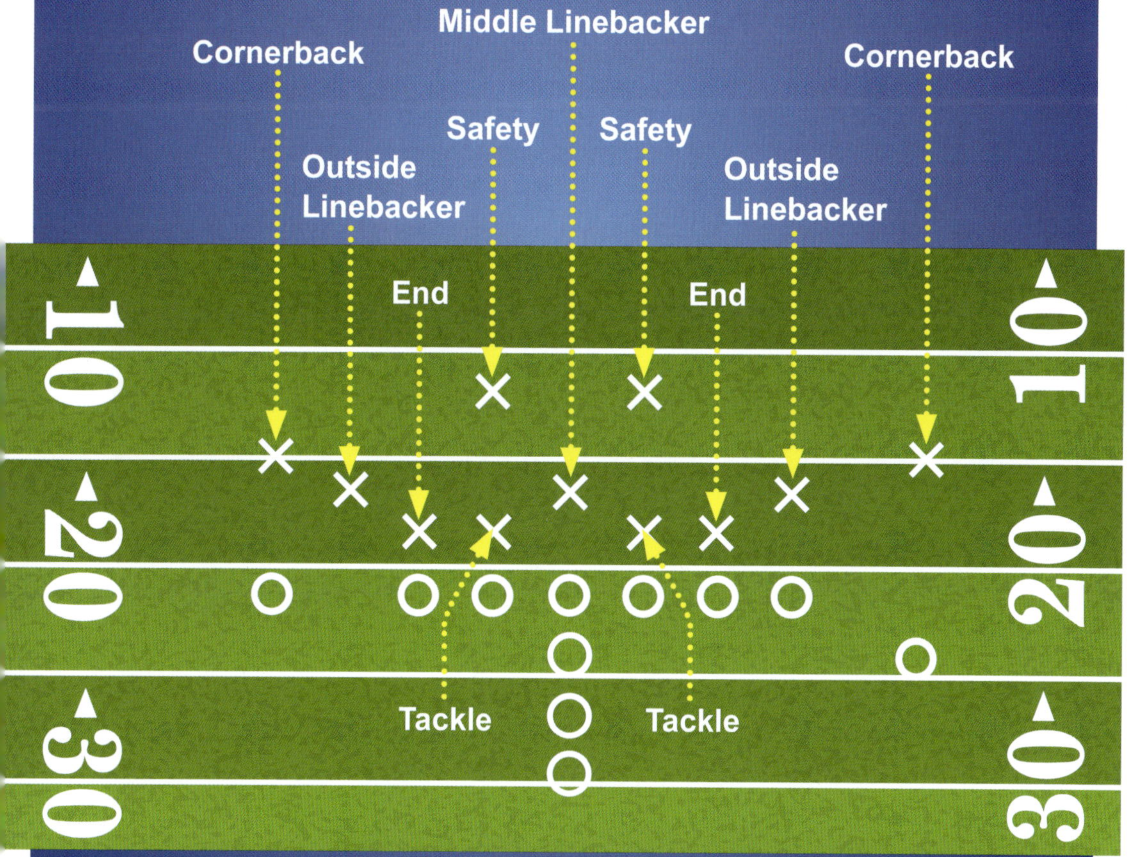

Eddie Jackson led the NFL with two interceptions returned for touchdowns in 2018.

Two players stand near the wide receivers. The ball is snapped. These players start running backward. They run with the receivers. They are the cornerbacks. Their job is to cover the receivers. Chicago had two good cornerbacks in Prince Amukamara and Kyle Fuller.

Two players stand in the center of the field. They are farthest away from the quarterback. These are safeties. They move farther back when the play starts. They are watching the ball. It is thrown to a receiver. Safety Eddie Jackson runs to the ball. He grabs it out of the air. Good safeties help slow down receivers. Players like Jackson are good at forcing **turnovers**.

CHAPTER 3

Lawrence Taylor was named NFL Defensive Player of the Year three times in his thirteen-year career.

All Sizes

Lawrence Taylor starts running at the quarterback. He chases him down. He slams him to the ground. Taylor was one of the greatest players of all time. He starred for the New York Giants. His best years came in the 1980s. Many consider Taylor to be the best defensive player in NFL history.

Fast forward to a few years later. Fans watched Reggie White play. He was bigger than Taylor. But he still got around linemen with no problem. He won a Super Bowl with the Green Bay Packers. Packers fans loved White. They cheered wildly when he **sacked** the quarterback.

NICKNAMES

Defenses have received many nicknames. Alan Page and Jim Marshall lined up for the Minnesota Vikings. They were part of a group called the Purple People Eaters. "Mean" Joe Greene was a star for the Pittsburgh Steelers. He was part of the Steel Curtain. Mike Singletary lined up for the Chicago Bears in the 1980s. He was one of the Monsters of the Midway.

Deion Sanders was an incredible athlete. He also played Major League Baseball.

It is the 1990s. Deion Sanders stands in his black Atlanta Falcons jersey. He is very close to a wide receiver. The ball is snapped. Sanders runs with the receiver. There is little room between the two. The quarterback throws to the receiver anyway.

The ball floats in the air. Sanders jumps up. Interception! Sanders starts running the other way. Sanders was one of the best defensive backs in the NFL. Teams were afraid to throw the ball near him.

TIMELINE OF TOP DEFENSIVE PLAYERS

1965

Dick Butkus, linebacker: Chicago Bears *(1965–73)*

"Mean" Joe Greene, defensive tackle: Pittsburgh Steelers *(1969–81)*

1975

Lawrence Taylor, linebacker: New York Giants *(1981–93)*

1985

Reggie White, defensive lineman: Philadelphia Eagles *(1985–92)*, Green Bay Packers *(1993–98)*, Carolina Panthers *(2000)*

Deion Sanders, cornerback: Atlanta Falcons *(1989–93)*, San Francisco 49ers *(1994)*, Dallas Cowboys *(1995–99)*, Washington Redskins *(2000)*, Baltimore Ravens *(2004–05)*

1995

Ed Reed, safety: Baltimore Ravens *(2002–12)*, New York Jets *(2013)*, Houston Texans *(2013)*

2005

J.J. Watt, defensive end: Houston Texans *(2011–)*

Khalil Mack, linebacker: Oakland Raiders *(2014–17)*, Chicago Bears *(2018–)*

2015

Troy Polamalu stands in the center of the field. His long hair bounces off his back. He sees the ball snapped. He looks around at the developing play. A wide receiver is running in the middle of the field. Polamalu gets close to him. The ball is thrown toward the receiver.

Polamalu launches himself. Boom! Polamalu runs into the wide receiver. The ball falls to the ground. Polamalu was one of the best defensive backs in NFL history. Pittsburgh Steelers fans loved watching him play in the 2000s.

FUN FACT

Polamalu was one of many NFL players of American Samoan descent.

Troy Polamalu was known for his long hair and his big hits.

CHAPTER 4

Aaron Donald led the NFL in sacks in 2018 with 20.5.

Today's Speedsters

Aaron Donald comes flying up the middle. He throws down the quarterback. Donald is one of the best defensive tackles in the league. He plays for the Los Angeles Rams. Donald is big and strong. But he is also fast. He runs quickly to the ball. Teams run away from Donald. He was named the NFL's Defensive Player of the Year in 2018. It was the second time he won that award.

Bobby Wagner stands near the ball. The ball is snapped. Wagner sprints toward the quarterback. He gets by one blocker. He runs straight into the quarterback. It's a sack!

The ball hits the ground. Wagner sees it. He jumps on it. Wagner is one of the NFL's best linebackers. He causes problems for offenses. He leads the Seattle Seahawks defense.

The quarterback throws a pass high in the air. He's looking for a receiver down the field. But he's covered by two players. One of those is Harrison Smith of the Minnesota Vikings. He leaps in the air. He grabs the ball with two hands. Interception! Safeties like Smith are hard to find. He's quick and can make game-changing plays.

FUN FACT

There are two types of safety: free safety and strong safety.

BOBBY WAGNER

CAREER STATS

Through the 2018 season

GAMES PLAYED	103
SACKS	16.5
TACKLES	591
TOUCHDOWNS	4
FORCED FUMBLES	4

Denzel Ward (21) blocks a field goal attempt in a 2018 game.

Denzel Ward of the Cleveland Browns runs backward. He is right next to the receiver. The receiver wants the ball. But the quarterback throws it to another player. The quarterback is afraid of Ward. Ward is one of the most exciting young defensive backs in the league.

Defense can play a role in every game. Players continue to get faster. They are also stronger. They will keep making it tough for offenses to score. Fans are excited to see the next great group of defenders.

BEYOND

THE BOOK

After reading the book, it's time to think about what you learned. Try the following exercises to jumpstart your ideas.

THINK

DIFFERENT SOURCES. Think about what types of sources you could find on the 2018 Chicago Bears defense. What could you find in a news article? What could you learn from the Bears website? What about an interview with a sports writer? How could each of the sources be useful in its own way?

CREATE

SHARPEN YOUR RESEARCH SKILLS. This book talks about great defensive players like Reggie White. Where could you go in the library to find more information about White? Who could you talk to who might know more? Create a research plan. Write a paragraph about your next steps.

SHARE

WHAT'S YOUR OPINION? In Chapter Two, it says that a defense is good when the entire group works together. Do you agree or disagree with this opinion? Use evidence from the text to support your answer. Share your position and evidence with a friend. Does your friend agree with you?

GROW

REAL-LIFE RESEARCH. What places could you visit to learn more about defensive backs? What other things could you learn while you were there?

RESEARCH NINJA

Visit www.ninjaresearcher.com/0745 to learn how to take your research skills and book report writing to the next level!

RESEARCH

DIGITAL LITERACY TOOLS

SEARCH LIKE A PRO
Learn about how to use search engines to find useful websites.

FACT OR FAKE?
Discover how you can tell a trusted website from an untrustworthy resource.

TEXT DETECTIVE
Explore how to zero in on the information you need most.

SHOW YOUR WORK
Research responsibly—learn how to cite sources.

WRITE

GET TO THE POINT
Learn how to express your main ideas.

PLAN OF ATTACK
Learn prewriting exercises and create an outline.

DOWNLOADABLE REPORT FORMS

Index

PHOTO CREDITS

The images in this book are reproduced through the courtesy of: Daniel Gluskoster/AP Images, front cover (left); Michael McGinnis/AP Images, front cover (center), p. 3; Greg Trott/AP Images, front cover (right); EFKS/Shutterstock Images, front cover (background); dean bertoncelj/Shutterstock Images, pp. 4, 19 (football), 24; Ben Liebenberg/AP Images, p. 5; Kathy Williens/AP Images, pp. 6–7; Perry Knotts/AP Images, pp. 8–9; Joseph Sohm/Shutterstock Images, p. 9; David Banks/AP Images, pp. 10–11, 14–15; Ryan Kang/AP Images, p. 12; Red Line Editorial, pp. 13, 19 (timeline), 25 (chart); Richard Cavalleri/Shutterstock Images, p. 15; Kathy Kmonicek/AP Images, p. 16; Al Messerschmidt/AP Images, p. 18; Gene J. Puskar/AP Images, pp. 20–21; Hiro Ueno/Los Angeles Rams/AP Images, pp. 22–23; Paul Abell/AP Images, p. 25 (Bobby Wagner); David Richard/AP Images, pp. 26–27; Olga Bogatyrenko/Shutterstock Images, p. 27; zieusin/Shutterstock Images, p. 30.

ABOUT THE AUTHOR

Kevin Frederickson is a freelance writer and editor from Ohio. He lives near Cincinnati with his golden doodle, Max.